YOUR LIFE MATTERS

YOUR LIFE MATTERS

ELIJAH STEVENSON

Copyright © 2025 by Elijah Stevenson

All rights reserved. No part of this book may be reproduced in any manner whatsoever without written permission except in the case of brief quotations embodied in critical articles and reviews.

First Printing, 2025 by Ingram Spark.

First published 2025 by Bekker Media on behalf of All That Entertainment.
ISBN: 978-1-7641247-1-3
EISBN: 978-1-7641247-2-0

Elijah Stevenson, *Your Life Matters*, National Library of Australia.

CONTENTS

ACKNOWLEDGEMENTS   vii
INTRODUCTION   ix

1. FORGIVENESS   1
2. COLD SHOWERS   9
3. MARTIAL ARTS   15
4. CREATIVE EXPRESSION   23
5. SOBRIETY   31
6. RESPONSIBILITY   37
7. CLEAN HOME   43
8. LISTEN   47
9. HONESTY   51
10. "CHALLENGE ACCEPTED"   57
11. BE A GOOD PERSON   63
12. ARE YOU READY TO RUMBLE   71
13. SHOOT YOUR SHOT   79
14. CLOSING WORDS   85

ACKNOWLEDGEMENTS

I would like to start by thanking my beautiful wife Nina. Her belief in me has been unparalleled. I know that no matter what endeavour I embark on, she not only has my back but truly believes I can do whatever needs to be done. I couldn't have come this far in life without a wife as solid and supportive as her.

Secondly, this book would not have been possible without the guidance and tutelage of Mr Anton Bekker. Anton inspired me to start writing around eight years ago when we first met at one of his Strategic Management Planning Days. He showed our group how to write a book and suggested everyone should write one. This was the beginning of a long and fruitful relationship with him as my closest mentor. No matter what project I am working on, I know I can ask for words of wisdom or guidance and rely on him for a discerning ear, uplifting critique and an unbiased conversation on any given topic.

I am also deeply grateful for my community. They say it takes a village to raise a child and I am no exception. After years of being a hindrance to my community to being fully backed by them, their forgiveness, love and understanding, has been nothing shy of a miracle.

Last but not least, I am truly blessed by God. His favour in my life can only be described as supernatural and my family and I have experienced a steady stream of miracles. Coming back to God in 2022 was the best thing that has happened to me, period. In the past three years I have gone from shouldering my burdens and fears on my own, to living a life of faith. He has been my Provider and Protector. He has been my Father and Counsellor. Even when life hits me like Mike Tyson's uppercuts, I can sit in a quiet peace I call Shalom, because I know God is not only with me but is working things out for me. I no longer live in fear of money or any type of scarcity because I know, no matter what, God is with me.

INTRODUCTION

As you read through this book, its purpose is to help guide you in making informed decisions about the steps you can take to create a life that is truly unique—one that sets you apart from the pack.

Life is the result of many small wins accumulated over time—and the reverse is also true. Small negative choices, though seemingly insignificant in the moment, can build up over time and eventually spiral beyond your control.

Each chapter in this book shares a life lesson I believe everyone should strive to live by. To give you deeper understanding, I've included the stories that led me to those lessons. I've watched people I love dearly fall into many of these traps, and it breaks my heart.

I often hear statements like, "Of course you're doing well—you didn't have it as hard as I did." Honestly, that kind of statement is complete nonsense. It's usually a defence mechanism to justify staying stuck in destructive patterns.

The truth is, my life has been far from easy—and I know many others who've had it even harder. But hardship should never be an excuse to settle for a life of mediocrity. That mindset is like a thief in the night, robbing you of the richness and potential life has to offer.

As a basic foundation, I believe this book will help lay a solid footing for your life. However, it is by no means a silver bullet. The work required of you is nothing short of a full-time job—and often, it comes with little recognition, especially in the beginning.

What this book *can* do is help shape you into a more pro-social individual—someone your community can rally behind and trust with real opportunities.

I hope this book finds its way into broken hearts and broken homes, bringing healing to young men, encouraging them to grow into great men, and ultimately making the world a better place—one man at a time.

CHAPTER 1

FORGIVENESS

> "Darkness cannot drive out darkness
> only light can do that,
> as hate cannot drive out hate
> only love can do that"
> **Dr Martin Luther King Jr**

Fuck, it's time to forgive them!

Who are you mad at?

Why?

Now let it go... Your mind no longer needs to stew in revenge, and your brain no longer needs to be a cesspit of resentment where people who aren't even thinking about you, live permanently rent free.

Growing up in a Christian household you would think I would have learned this early on - to forgive my enemies and turn the other cheek. At church on Sundays, I remember the sermons were long; nothing was ever relevant, and when I asked questions about the validity of the scriptures, I was usually given a canned answer such as, "That is where faith is needed." As a five-year-old asking these questions, this type of response created in me a bitter resentment and would later fill me with a violent rage.

My Mum was the sole provider for four beautiful kids, each with different fathers and a unique set of problems they would each have to face throughout their lives. My mum also went on to foster twenty-seven kids, many from broken homes, many of whom had been sexually abused or frequented the police station, if not prison. Now, my Mum was no saint and understandably so. From the age of five until sixteen, she had faced horrors that I wish upon no man. She was sexually assaulted and raped by her parents and some of her brothers until, at sixteen years old, she moved out and went to live with her grandmother to escape the horror show that had been her life. But she did not walk away unscathed. The traumatic experiences that shaped her formative years had split her personality into many pieces and like many abused children, she found herself battling addiction for many years to come.

"I'M JUST A PIECE OF SHIT, ASK MY KIDS THEY'LL TELL YOU," echoes from the empty bottles of rum after the shot glass is emptied only to be filled once more. As the screaming got louder, the details of her childhood abuse became more gruesome and vivid. The rest of the room remained silent, fearful of waking up more past memories, knowing that the resulting hatred would throw the moment into chaos.

"YOU DON'T KNOW WHAT IT'S LIKE TO HAVE YOUR MOTHER GET YOU DRUNK AND..."

Tears no longer formed in the ducts of my eyes, my mind grew quiet, and I would simply lie down, traumatised. That is when my soul grew cold, and my heart turned to stone. I understand why my mum acted in such a way and believe me when I say, when she was not drinking, she was the most caring loving parent anyone could ask for. She always tried to be the mother she wished she had as a kid—a mother who would never turn her back on her children. In our home, there were no secrets, no closed doors. We could come to her with any problem, whether it was sex, drugs, or any other ways we messed up. We always had a home to come back to and an open heart.

I have no doubt that the emotional scaring my mother endured rubbed off on us kids. I also knew it wasn't necessarily her fault. It was the fault of the criminals who abused her as a child. In saying that, I also knew it was her responsibility to deal with the hand that life had dealt her because no one else could do it for her, and if she didn't, she would keep hurting those around her. A large part of the heartbreak for me was that after a rum-fuelled night of yelling and screaming at us, she would not remember the next morning. This made things worse because she had no idea she was even hurting us, and this left a bitter taste in the air.

"With great sorrows of the night under the cities' skies, I became grateful for the few stars I could see in the polluted skies" (Elijah Stevenson)

The hardships we faced growing up had a silver lining - our family was brought together as tightly as could be. After all, we were all we had. It was just Mum, my brothers, my sister and me, no one else. We have quite a large extended family with many uncles, aunties and many cousins who were all estranged.

At some point, our tight-knit family unit also fell to pieces. I had made some foolish decisions and let my anger and ability to hold a grudge get the better of me. As a result, I spent some time behind bars for fighting. In my eyes, I thought what I had done was honourable, and the victim of my unchecked anger was more than deserving of what I had given him. Unfortunately, the courts decided that, as this was the third time I had faced them for fighting, I would have to spend some time locked up. Little did I know then that this would be the lynchpin that would lead to a brand-new life unfolding.

After a short stay in jail, I went on to move in with some friends. Then, shortly after, I lived in my car 'till I found myself nearly two thousand kilometres away from where I started, in a youth refuge for the homeless. In my travels, I had found a small red book written by Dr Martin Luther King Jr. I wasn't the best reader and had very little confidence doing so. I began reading this little red book. It was laid out very simply, making each page easy reading for a beginner. Each chapter was broken down into even smaller chapters; so, every time I finished a small part, I felt I had accomplished something. This made the book very enjoyable to read. Dr King's book gave me insights into the human psyche and explored a philosophy of a non-violent approach to a world that held many challenges you had to face, in most cases unjustly.

A section that stood out to me more so than any other was his depiction of the racism that had had the dark-skinned Americans living in fear. He did not say that those committing these appalling acts of hatred were bad people; a statement which nowadays may very well leave you at the mercy of cancel culture. Dr King went on to say that many of these people were good people, some pillars of the community who were very loving and caring people by nature. It was not their personality or character that was at fault, but their education. Over many years they had been sold the narrative that darker skinned people were primitive, or 'less-than'. The antidote to this hatred was, in fact, not rioting and hatred but one of love and understanding for those who had fallen victim to the heinous words that had shaped the beliefs. This process would take time and patience and would not happen overnight or, in Dr King's case, his lifetime. Each day, I believe we get a little closer to King's dream.

I harboured a tonne of hatred and anger. In many cases, I was no better than my mum. I would also take my anger out on other people. I truly didn't believe I was doing anything wrong—much to my dismay, I simply didn't know any better. After being estranged from my family for about one year, I began to miss them. I was very alone and would go several days without speaking to anyone in my day-to-day life, regularly checking in with myself asking, *"Have I said anything today?"* I lived a quiet life, which often worked against me. When faced with people who would only talk about drama or small-minded things, like gossip or the latest celebrity news, I tended to withdraw. This would usually exclude me from social groups, further isolating me from others. On the other hand, I did have a handle on introspection and understanding myself and my motivations, which later opened the door for me to face the demons of the past that lurked behind my mask.

Sitting by the beach deep in thought one afternoon, I reflected on my family situation and weighed up the pros and cons of having my family back in my life. The biggest con was the heartache which lingered in the air from the past. The pros mainly focused on the good times and love we shared. We were not a picture-perfect family, but we were all we had. Anything worthwhile was worth fighting for.

I decided to let my big sister and two little brothers back into my life, with boundaries. It was hard for me to let my mum back in because, depending on if she had been drinking or not, I didn't know which person I was going to be interacting with - the loving caring Mum or the resentful, hating screams-for-her-past Mum. I meditated for a long time on this, sitting down by the water's edge at night, letting my thoughts come and go like the crashing of the waves.

I woke up to a nice day and decided to clean up my one-bedroom flat which I had moved into temporarily as a part of the transitional housing program from the homeless refuge where I was staying. I browsed through the internet to see if I could find a phone number, and just like that, I found what I was looking for: my grandparents' home phone number. For many years I had envisioned our next encounter - it was usually an uncontrolled attack, with me physically assaulting them for what they had done to my mother and the pain they had caused her. This usually produced a chain reaction that left me somewhat damaged.

I dialled the number, each number harder to press than the last. My finger hovered over the green telephone symbol, adrenaline pumping through my entire body. The phone started to ring. *Ring, ring, ring, ring.* It felt like it rang forever. Just as I began to assume no one would answer, an older women answered:

"Hello?" she softly enquired.

"O, hey," I replied. "I don't know if you remember me. My name is Elijah. I am Julie's son."

My heart, at this point, was beating uncontrollably. She assured me she remembered me and asked, "How are you doing?"

I responded, "I am well. How are you?"

She said she was "Doing okay."

I began to explain why I had called, "I was forgiving my mother for the pain she had caused me and my siblings throughout our lives, but I could not forgive Mum without first forgiving you."

In what sounded like a state of shock, her silence broke with, "Okay."

I asked if she knew what I was talking about, and she replied with, "Yes, I think so."

"A waterfall crashes in a chaotic scene, but too often we forget the waters pass through many domains before it reaches the bottom of the cliff" (Elijah Stevenson)

I went on to say, "Not only do I forgive you and Mum, but wherever this pain originated from, I forgive them, too." I decided it was going to end with me; as Dr Martin Luther King Jr had said, "Love is the only thing that can defeat hatred."

I had to ask my grandmother one last question, "Do you love my mother...." and to my surprise, she responded, "I will always love your mother, but it does not mean I have to like her," and on that note, I hung up the phone.

As I walked around the front yard, I felt lighter. In fact, I felt weightless. I genuinely felt my feet lift from the ground as a light grew inside of me. As I hovered in this euphoric state, I truly understood the depth of what I had done. My mind was at peace. I felt illuminated. I had just released over twenty years of hatred and resentment, and for the first time in my life I was free—free from my mother's pain and the generational pain that pervaded my family.

Forgiveness can have so much utility in your every day-to-day life. If I can muster the courage to forgive my extended family for the wrong things they did, I am sure you can forgive those who have hurt you.

There is no point in being a vessel for revenge and hate. Hate in itself is a destructive force and because of this, it tends to self-sabotage – which is why I landed up in jail. Even little things in our lives sometimes get to us, but it is our responsibility to face them and deal with them appropriately. Otherwise, we are creating an inner world that accepts our own shortcomings as the future, and this leaves our children vulnerable to our mistakes.

So, I'll ask you one more time and really think about each question:

Who are you mad at?

Why?

Would you let it go if given the chance?

When would you let it go?

The answer is RIGHT NOW.

CHAPTER 2

COLD SHOWERS

"Life isn't about waiting for the storm to pass...
It's about learning to dance in the rain."
Vivian Greene

So, there I was, tired, run down, and unproductive.

The best thing in my world at this point was that my beautiful daughter has just been born, despite the interrupted nights and lack of sleep. On a quest to pick myself up, I had worked myself into the ground. To become something more than I was at the time, I was trying to replicate the hyper successful entrepreneurs on line, with their savage daily routines.

I had watched several videos that suggested that caffeine may be the cause of the problem. They discussed fact that it caused adrenal fatigue and promised more energy and productivity if you quit this habit.

Day 1: I slept and that's about it.

Day 2: I was working all day with a headache from the minute I opened my eyes 'till the minute I closed them. It was truly horrible.

For the next week or so, I was sluggish and didn't really want to do anything. After nearly three months, I was convinced I had been sold a lie. There were a great deal of positives to a life without caffeine. For example, I was in a constant state of calm, which was very pleasant, but it was a double-edged sword. That little jitter that lies under the skin after having a cup of coffee is what had pushed me to be productive and to outperform myself and get things done. Without caffeine I became lazy.

Prior to quitting caffeine, I had a series of daily tasks I would aim to accomplish every day, and most days I would do okay with my list. Other days, I would look at how I was feeling and say, "You know what? Not today. I'm beat." Usually however, I felt bad about not giving it my best shot. One of the things I would aim to do every day was have a cold shower. I started this practice several years ago after stumbling across Wim "the-ice-man" Hoff on-line one day. At face value it seemed like a great thing to try. Some of the appeal of taking daily cold showers was its effect on inflammation in the body. As a martial artist, I am regularly covered in bruises and have muscle soreness and various other injuries, some worse than others. So, it began - whether it was hot or cold outside, I was in the cold shower religiously, every day. As winter settled in, I didn't even notice until I saw everyone else was wearing jumpers, beanies, gloves and scarves. I had become unaffected by the cold winter temperatures. That's cool.

Not long after I began to practice cold exposure, I noticed my skin and hair began to look a lot nicer, and I had more confidence in myself. I felt like I was accomplishing something by doing something only a small amount of people dare to try. People often say to me, "O, you're mad, having a cold shower in the middle of winter!" To which, I usually reply with, "Winter is the best time, because the water is finally cold enough for me."

It is not an easy thing to jump into the freezing cold by any stretch of the imagination. The internal battle of whether to jump or not is one I fought daily, but with each cold shower you get stronger, braver, and more willing to face not only the cold but also the voice in your mind that tells you it is too dangerous or to scary. Being in the cold is like jumping into the pool on a hot day. You're hesitant at first, but once you're in and you get used to the cold water, it's not as bad as you had thought.

There are a lot of studies done on cold exposure and its benefits to the body and mind. It helps relieve depression and is a great tool to combat arthritis. You can go on-line and find a list of benefits quite easily, with links to the research. But the two biggest benefits I have found after doing this for so long is:

1. It builds your willpower. Willpower is a muscle, and the more you work on it, the stronger it gets. I regularly have people say to me: *How do you do so much? I am always so tired, or I have no time.* I am confident that it's safe to say that being disciplined in this practice will build your mindset to accomplish more things than you had ever thought possible. It is not only the willpower to have a cold shower you strengthen, but also the willpower to overcome any obstacle you may encounter in the future.

2. I had trained my brain through the constant cold exposure, to not only answer but overcome any obstacle in my way, including excuses.

For me personally, I found the excuses I made to not have a cold shower were the same excuses I used to say why I "couldn't" do a lot of things I wanted to. They were literally recycled excuses.

In the beginning of this chapter, I spoke about feeling burnt out, tired, and unproductive. But what I failed to mention was that I was happier than I had ever been. My life was going great. I was engaged to an amazing woman. I had just had a baby girl whom I adored, work life was flourishing, and so was my social life. I had everything I had ever wanted. I became content. The hard work I had invested into myself over the years was paying off. Yet, something was wrong. At this point, I was taking more hot showers every day because, just like everyone else, I enjoyed the comfort. The nice hot water on a cold morning; what's not to love?

I assured myself a hot shower's okay, and it is. Then I began to say: I am still having more cold showers than hot. I am good. Finally, it became very evident I had given up. I went from daily cold showers, ice baths, and cryotherapy chambers which were constant reminders of self-improvement, to just wanting a little comfort. Slowly, those same excuses that stopped me taking cold showers reared their heads in other areas of my life; and I had not noticed.

I had every right to feel tired and run down. I was working three jobs. My fiance and I had just had a baby and were in and out of hospital. I went to training nearly every night as I was working towards my black belt grading. On top of all that, I was trying to learn two languages, improve my maths and English, whilst studying a business course and God knows what else. And with each day my productivity dropped, and I missed one or two or, God forbid, everything on my list. I became defeated, depressed, and overwhelmed. This is when I decided the answer lay in the amount of coffee I drank.

I knew I had not taken my cold showers seriously in a long time, and so I decided to lighten my load and just try and start my days with a cold shower and see what happened. The first couple of days, I would end the hot shower with a minute or so of just cold water, mostly because I was scared to jump straight back in. The very first day after I had a cold shower again, I noticed the difference. I powered through the day, smashing out goals. and I finally felt alive again. Each day that passes now, I am reminded of the importance of getting out of your comfort zone. If you want to be exceptional, you have to do exceptional things every day. Over time, this is what will separate you from the pack.

I feel I have more willpower now than I ever had before, and I do believe it's because of having cold showers. Even when I am tired from getting up in the middle of the night or if I have had a terrible day, I know that as soon as I jump in a cold shower the only thing to worry about is the freezing cold water hitting your skin. Everything else disappears. They call this survival mode. Nothing else matters in that moment. This practice is especially valuable when you're feeling down and out or too comfortable for your own good; a cold shower a day will shake things up for you and give you a fresh start.

CHAPTER 3

MARTIAL ARTS

"The ultimate aim of martial arts is not having to use them."
Miyamoto Musashi

Since a young kid, I have been fascinated with fighting - the act of being a dangerous person. I felt this person demanded a certain degree of respect from his peers or would at least strike fear in the hearts of those who choose to go against him. I was no stranger to fighting. Growing up, my first fight is still so vivid in my memory.

I must have been six or seven years old, and a friend and I were walking around school, talking, when the topic of whether or not we had ever been in a fight came up. We both confessed we had not been in one yet and really wanted to. So, we agreed we would have a fight. Like a series of flashing images, I remember how we began to grapple and throw punches until we fell to the ground, struggling to overpower each other.

Then we heard a sound.

"HEY!!, What do you think you are doing?" Mrs Batt yelled from above the walkway, with shock and disbelief on her face. "To the principal's office, now!" she demanded, and in a split second it was over.

My friend and I shrugged it off. We didn't think we had done anything wrong. We had both decided to willingly enter into combat, but we did so as friends to help each other accomplish something neither of us had ever attempted before.

I would like to say I was a good fighter as a kid; with the number of stories I can tell, you would be forgiven to think I was. But at 5 ft nothing and less than 55kg right up into my late teens and no formal training in martial arts, I had sloppy techniques. My punches did not do much damage, and I was usually much younger and smaller than my opponents, although these things rarely deterred me. There were a lot of kids in our neighbourhood and the majority of us lived below the poverty line. Criminal life in our families and peers was something we all shared in common. I had a very different mindset then to the one I have today.

I have come to realise that, more than anything, I admired dangerous men, men who could protect their families, their partners and kids; men that looked out for their own. I never relied on my friends being there for me in a fight. My heart and wanting to win would back me up, or so I thought. My friends had my back a lot of the time when I was in trouble.

As I came of age, I began to take more and more risks, not only by fighting but also by trying out criminal behaviour. A group of friends and I hung out in a dimly lit garage that I had converted into a bedroom; we would smoke cigarettes and drink and occasionally smoke the devil's lettuce. We decided we should have a fight night. We would pick a person in the room and fight them for nothing more than fun, and, I guess in hindsight, personal growth. I chose my friend Bob. Bob was a big boy, much taller than I was, and very heavy set. To my knowledge, he went on the be a security guard. Shocked that I had chosen to fight him, he agreed. Then just like that, I throw a right hook into his cheek, and that was it. He grabbed me in a bear hug and threw me to the ground, dominating me until someone broke us up. We all had plenty of fights that night, and some of us fought more than one person at a time. Fighting had become a part of my identity, even to the point where I gained the nickname "Tiger," as in the *Eye Of The Tiger* from the Rocky movie. I think I earned the nickname more for my heart than for being a good fighter. Even after being knocked out, I would still get up and continue.

I guess I held myself differently as time went on. Now, when recounting my stories with others in new surroundings, they find it hard to believe but can tell I am telling the truth. The eyes are a window to the soul, and I have nothing to hide.

I was never sure why, but I moved to a small outback town in Queensland, Australia where I found myself accumulating many enemies, or at least people who just decided that I was public enemy number one, many of whom I had never even met. And from time to time, I would run into these people, and we would have it out. Sometimes I would get the better of them, and other times I would walk away worse off than the other guy, sometimes not even landing a single punch.

One night I met a young man at a pub that I frequented, and for whatever reason he decided that he was going to treat me like I was less than nothing, with no common courtesy. He also influenced others to do the same, some of whom I considered at the time to be my friends. So, for no reason at all, I was blacklisted. It took a lot for me to just walk away. Until one night, at a large event just out of town, I was having a hard time with this and decided to talk to him, knowing damn well he would treat me with nothing but disrespect.

I approached him and tried to be polite. "Hey, man, how you been?" As he grunted like a pig and literally stuck his nose up at me. I repeated, "What's been up? How's work going for you?"

Again, nothing but rude impolite gestures and responses from him. The others standing around began to treat me in the same way, and, just like that, I was a joke.

Grabbing the scruff of his shirt, I firmly said, "Hey, mate, I said how is work?"

Then, in a flurry I applied multiple strong right punches to his smug mouth. His body began to go limp, only supported by me holding him up by the scruff of his shirt. I let go. He fell back through the crowded area. As he hit the ground, I glanced at the others who thought it was okay to treat me with no human decency. I stepped over his unconscious body and walked away.

After being chased by a group of half a dozen or so of his friends five minutes later, I was escorted home by the local police officer. We sat in the police car and he asked what had happened. I told him the story, and he replied, "boys will be boys." I was not being charged unless the guy came in and laid charges. I apologised for making his job more difficult by causing such a ruckus. After several weeks, I relaxed as there were no charges laid, thinking that he had taken the beating like a man and owned his wrongdoing. At this point I was happy to let go of any animosity I harboured towards him.

Three and a half months later, I returned with my little brother from a holiday on the Gold Coast where we had spent time with friends letting our hair down. I was getting ready to continue my bachelor's degree in Human Behaviour, which I had just started, and my brother went back to working on the local council. My phone rang, and it's the local police officer. "I'm sorry, Elijah", he reluctantly said to me, indicating that this was not what he wanted to tell me, "He has just come in and pressed charges against you for assault."

Just like that, my whole life changed. Within that week, the policed received a tip off that I had been selling drugs out of my house, which at this point in my life could not have been further from the truth. My home was raided by police who found these drugs I had allegedly been selling.

As my court date approached, I spoke with a close friend, who gave me a piece of advice that has stuck with me all these years. I give it to others who are being foolish in their decisions, "It's time that you wise up," he said, "get yourself a lawyer. This is your third assault charge. You're going to jail."

And I did just that. The first law firm I contacted agreed to represent me. But as they asked me questions, it seemed they were trying to paint me as a mentally ill danger to society. As the conversation continued, I found out that the lawyer in question was a close friend of the victim's family. I realised they were not there to help me. It was a small town. Everyone knew everyone, and I was not very well liked at this point. Only a few people stood by me through this, and these people were the older men who were hard, old-school men. I had always admired them because they stood up for what they believed, despite what other people said.

I ended up getting a lawyer from a town over 200 kilometres away who represented me quite well. On a six-month sentence, I was to serve three or four weeks behind bars. Prison was not what I expected. Each unit was segregated by race to keep the peace, and the unit I was in was almost like a halfway unit, as people would eventually leave and be placed accordingly. So, there was no segregation. I was sussed out by both blacks and whites regularly, each with their own questions and each with their own perks. Fights happened almost daily and somehow no one saw anything, mostly because if you rock the ship, you get tossed out. The aboriginal guys took a liking to me, more so than the white guys, which resulted in me getting a better cell, a better mattress, and a great deal of perks for which I am quite grateful for. This made my time in prison much easier than it could have been. It was being in jail that made me realise that I had to work out daily and quit smoking cigarettes to not only get stronger and fitter, but healthier.

After I was released, I found myself back on the central coast of New South Wales, Australia, where I had grown up. After living in my car for close to a year, I was still working out daily. Once I found some stability in the homeless refuge, I drove past a martial arts gym MUNEN MUSO Martial Arts. They offered everything: karate, jiu-jitsu, boxing, Muay Thai, MMA, Krav Maga. In that moment I knew that I was meant to train there. I walked in and spoke with the owner behind the counter about starting classes. It was quite funny; he made jokes about if my payments were late, they would have to give me a beating.

I began to take the MMA classes and Muay Thai to start off with and without even knowing it, I went from aimlessly cruising through life to finding purpose. I had always believed that somewhere in my family history there was a gladiator or a warrior that I felt the remnants of in my soul and believed that was why I had a proclivity for fighting and danger.

I was a very angry man. I was mad at my family as I felt they had not done all they could have done to heal their own wounds which they then handed down to my siblings and me. I was mad because I grew up without a father in my life. I was mad that every time I tried to get my life together, I would end up on the streets and alone. As I took my aggression out on the heavy bags and, my favourite, the ground and pound bag, I was fuelled by the rage, the power it gave me. I would train four hours a night, some nights attending class after class. I feel sorry for some of my training partners who felt the heat of this aggression some nights, but it's a combat sport after all. I began to get quite good at martial arts as time progressed. I wasn't anything special, but I was consistent; come rain, hail, or shine, and through blood, sweat, and tears, I was there. Whether I had a car or not, or whether I was homeless again, or had other obligations, I was there at the gym, ready to train.

One day, I noticed that I wasn't as fired up as usual to train and smash the hell out of everything in my path. I wasn't sure what had happened until it hit me, and it hit me hard. I was no longer angry.... I had no desire to smash things. Even when faced with hostile situations outside the gym, when I would normally have fought, I had no desire to. I was at peace.

At the time I was watching an anime series called *The Last Airbender*, and I am honestly grateful I was when this happened. In the TV series the bad guy is powered by his rage and anger. Once he is no longer angry, he can't understand why he has lost all his powers and can no longer bend the fire to destroy. He learns that anger is not a sustainable fuel source for his martial arts, or in his life. He realises that he will get better results by living a good life and practising with discipline and consistency rather than anger. It takes him a while, but he becomes a better martial artist as a result and is much happier for it. I guess you could say I went through the same metamorphosis as the villain in this cartoon series.

I am now a much better fighter than I have ever been in my life. I am stronger than I ever was, but I don't want to fight any more, unless, touch wood, I have to. I live a clean, stress-free life of forgiveness and understanding now, and although I feel I can handle myself in a conflict, I have become far more diplomatic in these scenarios, allowing myself to remain calm and to take the high road instead. I still love the sport of MMA and love fighting, but now I do it because it fulfils a yearning desire in me, not to destroy as fire engulfs everything in its path.

CHAPTER 4

CREATIVE EXPRESSION

"Creativity is a way to share my soul with the world"
Brene Brown

My lead pencil lightly rubbed against the paper as my model, the classmate next to me, looked on.

In 3rd grade our art teacher instructed us to draw the person next us. As a young boy I loved drawing. I would sit in the library, pulling out book after book on the shelf learning how to draw in my spare time.

I was loving the experience of drawing a real person. I put my heart and soul into a realistic portrait of my friend Stephan. I remember looking at his drawing of me - a very simple drawing, an odd-shaped circle for a head, two semi circles for ears, the kind of thing you would expect a kid of our age to draw. As I worked on my drawing, I took note of the intricate swirls in the ears, the ratio of the eyes, nose, and mouth, and how they were positioned on the face. I would go on to spend a lot of time, adding details like getting the hair perfect and all the shading correct to bring my drawing to life.

The end of class approached, and the teacher collected each student's piece of art they had created. She began to show each individual piece and complement them, saying what a good job this student had done and what a marvellous effort that student had done. You could imagine the drawings a class of Third Graders would produce. So, I was really excited for the class and the teacher to see my artwork and hear the kind words she had said about all the others which were much less advanced than mine. She flicked through the drawings, and my picture pops up. She says quite softly and without enthusiasm, "and Elijah…" I waited for some sort of praise or acknowledgment for my hard work and study. It never came. She just said "and Elijah …" My poor little heart was broken. "Was it bad? Did I do something wrong?" Self-doubt spewed in. Maybe I wasn't as good as I thought. At this stage I identified with art and drawing. I had devoted a lot of time and effort learning and improving my craft, and for what? Maybe I wasn't an artist after all.

Five years later, I went to High School. At this point, I was heavily influenced by hip hop and gangster rap. I was drawn to rap music and graffiti like a bee to honey. These rappers got it. They knew what it was like growing up poor, not knowing when you were going to eat or if the lights would get shut off. They lived in very similar conditions, where drugs and crime were just a part of life, and as a young man it was more likely you would be in jail or dead by the time you were twenty-five, rather than have a career or some sort of white-collar success. All that was for the rich people, not people like us. One aspect I am grateful for and a big difference between me and the artists I looked up to, was that in Australia we didn't have guns. So, people didn't get shot every day; but we did have bats, knives, and fists and an overwhelming desire to be something good or bad.

I fell in love with graffiti. I would write the word *EPIC* as my calling card for those who had the eyes to see it. I chose this word because, from a young age, my mum always said to me, "God has a huge calling on your life", and "You will do great things". Regardless, whether you have a belief in God or not, being told you are something more than you could ever imagine is very empowering. My tag was a reflection of what I believed about myself and what I was capable of in the future, not today, but down the line. My books at school were filled with graffiti, from simple lettering to extravagant mural designs. I would incorporate all the things I had learned in my younger years into these pieces. I felt I was really good at this, and my friends agreed. They gave me the confidence to pursue my art. They believed in me and loved my drawings, and just like that, my confidence in my art was back. But it was still very limited. I was scared to stray from street art, because I thought: I am good at graffiti but not really too much else.

I soon began imitating my favourite rappers, learning all their songs and singing along, then going on to trying to write my own lyrics. Back then, we would steal CDs from the music store, mostly singles because they were easier to take. And on these singles the instrumental of the track was usually included. I don't know exactly where it came from, but we had an old tape cassette player, like an old school boom box which had a record function. We would pretend we were radio announcers, with our own shows, and laugh at how funny we sounded when we heard our own voices played back. My younger brother and I would write rap songs, songs to the instrumental beats from the singles, and record them on to the tape cassette. We were obviously the next big thing, like every other young person who found out they could do this.

I came of age and began noticing girls and dealing with puberty; a very confusing time for most young people. I would write the words that came to mind that would roughly describe how I was feeling. I have a distinct memory writing the word: "Confusing" in graffiti, my way of trying to make sense of what was happening. Although I could write a word as arbitrary as 'strawberries' and know exactly what it was and how it made me feel, no one else would have any idea that it was me, reflecting on a friend of mine who was really kind to me. The challenge then became how do I express myself to others in such a way that it truly shows how I feel and who I am. That is when I met a girl, a girl who I would fall for completely and who eventually broke my heart.

I began writing lyrics about how I felt about her. These became poems. One day I was brave enough to show her, and she loved it. She asked me to write more for her, so you would find me in my room after school, writing coming of age poems about being in love and how confusing this whole experience was for me. My heart began to break as we drifted apart. These love poems turned darker, and fewer poems were written. The desire to write and share my soul died. I felt like a man walking in a tunnel, blinded by the light of his heart, and as it grew dim, he realised there was no light at the end of the tunnel and no reason to love any more. I lost any belief that love was real and separated myself from the very idea.

I would go on to occasionally write in private, for my own eyes, mostly dark, heartless thoughts. I found myself writing in hard times about loneliness, murder, and sometimes suicide. I would go on to stop writing eventually and never shared any of my heart or my writings with anyone.

I was twenty-three years old and had gotten out of jail only to find myself living in my car for about a year. I ended up more than two thousand kilometres from the prison, in the town I grew up in. I stopped by the homeless kitchen to get something to eat and hopefully wash my clothes. I sat down at the table with a lot of familiar faces around me, many of whom had no idea who I was. As I was eating a hot meal prepared by the volunteers, a larger gentleman approached, slightly greyed black hair, dark skin, and a kind voice.

"I haven't seen you around here before. What is your story?"

This moment, right here, is a lynchpin in my life. His name was Dave; he was in charge of one of the homeless refuges on the Central Coast and asked if I would like a bed to sleep in?

I replied in shock, "What? Like tonight?"

He said, "Yeah".

I went back to the refuge, and he gave me the run down on the do's and don'ts and what was expected of me. I played ball and did the right thing; they would help get me into my own accommodation.

Dave and I became quite close. As I shared my stories with him, he would share his experiences with me. I began to look up to Dave quite a bit. While I was living in my car, I began to write again as a way to face my past head on. I figured if I could face my traumas, even if it was only through metaphors, I would be one step closer to dealing with the post-traumatic stress I had been suffering from for the past ten or so years. I asked Dave one day if I could share a poem with him, and he fully embraced the idea. The poem read along the lines of:

> *As he runs through the forest*
> *Troubled and entangled in the memories of danger*
> *He fronts an old enemy as a new stranger*
> *Slicing his already open wounds*
> *He is left for dead*
> *Thrown into the forest onto a flower bed*
> *He is devoured left feeling sour hour to hour*
> *Watching the world drift away as he is killed by the flowers*
> *Though innocent to the eye toxic inside*
> *Affecting everything around it as its victim dies*
> *Once it has touched its victim they will feel*
> *The connection as it courses through their veins*
> *It watches its own poison intensify*
> *As the trees around gather as it kills its victim*
> *They remind him that they are not listening*
> *As the pain draws closer as if it were never there*
> *He sees his soul holding more than it can bear*
> *As the trees look on protecting the flower*
> *Blood falls from the sky in a light shower*

The innocent victim now defending himself
As the trees gives cover for its companion's assault.
The prey has been caught in a forest full of lies and deceit
As he is turned to stone he finds it hard to breath
Growing limbs of memories seeing his pain
Now they are there they will not fade
He tries to escape but he is entrapped
Even for hope of help he has no luck
Takes one last look at what could have been
As his life is taken from him.

"Wow," Dave responded.

It may not have been this exact poem, but it was one very similar to this one. I was very surprised as Dave went on to encourage me to write more and also share with him more; so, I did. He said to me one day that I should really be doing something with my poems, and so I thought I could give it a go. I looked online for open mics and things of that nature. I came across a very welcoming community of New Age, hippie-type people who were more than happy to accommodate me and my poetry.

The open mic came around, and before I knew it, I was on the stage, trembling behind my phone screen on which I had written my poem. In a soft, quiet voice, I very quickly read the words in front of me. I was in a hurry to get off the stage, scared of the ridicule that could follow me baring my soul in front of complete strangers. I finished reciting. I looked at the crowd, and applause filled the air. As I left the stage, people congratulated me, complementing my poetry.

"Wow", I thought, but also, "Fuck!" It was way too full on, getting on stage and sharing my innermost thoughts and feelings with people.

I decided to give up, under the rationale that I was the only poet there and no one does poetry anyway. It's lame, etc. All the excuses I could muster came to mind. Until I saw a new venue had just opened not far from the open mic: "The Lounge Room", a social enterprise event space that raised money for disadvantaged youth.

Low and behold, they were having an open mic poetry night. So naturally intrigued, I went along.

The night came along, and I had a new piece to recite. I had my $5 for the entry fee, and I walked into a place that smelled of freshly roasted coffee grounds and mix of hip-hop and R&B played through the speakers. "Yo, Yo, Yo, thank you all for coming," and just like that, I had found my tribe.

I went on to learn the tools of the trade from some of the best people, while at the same time helping out wherever I could and volunteering for the charity as well. I shared my soul, my heartaches, and my sorrow with hundreds of people, and went on to become a headlining act. I also started doing poetry workshops, teaching others how to write poetry.

One day I realised the pain and sorrow that fuelled my writing had left. A quote came to me: "I will have to scratch my scars so I can bleed once more". I was happy, confident and no longer had space in my mind for such darkness.

I still write poetry now, but poems of love and growth, poems for my wife and my daughter, poems of overcoming hardships and walking with purpose into a better life. Sometimes I write just to share my views on things, especially when my thoughts are not the same as everyone else.

Art and poetry need to be nurtured and encouraged. It is equally important not to seek external validation to tell you whether you are good at it or not. Art is used to open deep wounds of the past and heal them. It is a way to share your spirit with the world, and if you're lucky enough to be around people who want to listen and encourage you to express yourself, then you should do just that. You may just shine the light needed for somebody who is in desperate need of those words or inspire others to begin writing as well.

One of my favourite poems is a short one on altruism, and I think we would be wise to love ourselves as such.

"THE SUN RISES AND GIVES TO OUR HEARTS REGARDLESS."
(ELIJAH STEVENSON)

CHAPTER 5

SOBRIETY

*"Wine is a mocker and beer a brawler;
whoever is led astray by them is not wise."*
Proverbs 20:1

I was probably around eleven or twelve years old.

Crazy Yvonne (who we named due to her habit of mowing her lawn in nothing but a G-string whilst talking to herself) left a carton of Victoria Bitters (beers) on her porch.

I and the other neighbourhood boys decided we should probably just take that for ourselves, and for some of us it would be our first time drinking alcohol. We snuck along the fence where the overgrown shrubs gave us some cover and as little sneak thieves, crouched down and began to approach the target. Once it was snatched, there was a mad dash to the fence line where another friend waited to receive the beer on the other side. We did it! We had successfully stolen some beer from an old woman with mental health problems...

Later that day we met up in the bush along the fence of a friend's house. This seemed to be the best place to enjoy our spoils from our mission. I remember very clearly questioning my best friend at the time, who was several years older than me, about the effects of drinking as I had never done it before. He said, "Just let me know if you feel weird". I opened the warm bottle of beer and began to drink the foul beverage, pretending I was actually enjoying it, because truth be told, I just wanted to be part of the moment. Not even one bottle down and my head began to spin. "Wow, what's going on?" I immediately turned to my friend and said, "I think I am feeling it." He immediately asked me to stop and walked me home. From that moment on, we began drinking more and more regularly.

Not long after this experience, one of the neighbourhood boys found some alcohol lying around and drank himself unconscious. I remember his dad being terrified and, not knowing what had happened or what to do, put him in a cold shower to cool him down while he called the ambulance. This poor young boy, who was younger than me, was taken to hospital with alcohol poisoning and had to have his stomach pumped. Surely this would have been a wake-up call to us young boys, but as life would have it, this did not even remotely act as a deterrent.

I would drink quite frequently after this, well into my early twenties. In hindsight I would say that in most cases when I was involved in violence, crime, or general deviant behaviour, I was either drinking or about to. At twenty-three years of age, I stumbled around the countryside, occasionally having enough money to stay in some budget accommodation, which at this particular time of my life happened to be a not-so-classy pub. This was my second stay in that hotel. The first time I had stayed in a small room, maybe four meters by four meters. The room had no windows, a bed, and a bedside table. This time, I was fortunate enough to have room with a balcony that overlooked the main street of the town. Although the upgrade was a nice change, to give you some idea of the place I was staying - my front door looked as if it had been kicked in several times, and the framework of the doorway had been damaged by blunt force or from prying it open.

The next-door neighbour was an older gentleman who seemed to have more influence over the hotel and its residents than anyone else. He also had a sixteen-year-old girl who lived with him. The general smell of the place was one of marijuana, cigarettes, and alcohol. As was the case with most derelict places I had lived before, there was an untold law of see no evil, speak no evil, and hear no evil. Consequently, if there was any shady business going on, no one saw anything, and it was none of your business.

I sat on my balcony alone one evening with a box of cheap white wine and some soft drink to take the bitterness off the soured grapes. I had some plastic cups, the kind you use once at a picnic and then throw out. Sitting there alone got me thinking: "What if I was thirty and I was still sitting here drinking alone?" My mind blew open and began to frighten me, "What if I was forty?" I began to get anxious. "What if I was fifty?" The thought scared the life out of me. I finished my plastic cup of wine mixed with cheap soft drink. I would like to say that I never drank again, but it would be a lie. Now that I had seen what my future could be if I stayed on the path I was on, I began to be chased by the demons the future had in-store for me.

'Dry July' came along not long after this realisation, and I thought this would be a good start. I took up the challenge: one month with no alcohol. It wasn't too bad. I landed a job on a fishing boat before too long and was able to sleep on the boat, which was a nice change to sleeping in my car. The general culture of the Australian fisherman is one of drinking. You work hard during the day and drink at night, and when you get back from sea, you continue to drink until you leave port again. So, when I showed up and refused to drink, it was received as quite the shock, but nonetheless, respected. I do have a slight suspicion that one of the reasons it was socially accepted in this case was because it was Dry July, and it was only for a month. One month later, I congratulated myself on my accomplishment with an ice-cold beer. The first sip "Ahhh." It was very refreshing. The second, not so much, and by the third sip I felt my mind being dulled and I felt as if I had lost my mental acuity. So, I put the beer down and chose to not finish it.

After returning from sea, I chose to only drink on special occasions like birthdays, Christmas etc. One night, some local fisherman, some of whom I had never met, invited me out for some beers at the beach. The deal was sweetened by the offer of a room to stay in, instead of the boat. The night started off quite pleasantly. I had a bottle of water, which I would refill through the night, and no one was urging me to drink or do drugs. One fisherman caught wind of my discipline and tried to destroy, or at least test, my commitment. He began to offer me beer after beer, which I politely refused and reply with, "I'm okay with water". The man in question stood maybe 6.4 feet and weighed maybe 120 kilograms, a much larger man than me. His girlfriend approached me and told me that he said he was going to make me drink by the end of the night and that she had seen him do it before. This did not bother me in the slightest as I knew that my decision was made, and I wasn't going to back-flip on it.

The fisherman began to offer me free drinks and then, before I could say no thanks, he would say, "Actually, you can't have it", as if to apply some sort of reverse psychology on me. To me, this was laughable. These kinds of antics continued on through the night, until he had had enough of me saying no. So, he grabbed me by the neck and forced a drink to my face and demanded I drink. I pushed him away, and my first instinct was to kick him in his ribs with a round house. Just like that, without thinking or debating, my leg left the ground and hit him in the floating ribs. He looked at me in shock as if to say, "I didn't deserve that!" The onlookers sided with their long-time friend and made it clear I was the problem. None of the fisherman escalated the situation after this, but made it very clear I was no longer welcome, and I'd better find somewhere else to stay. So, I calmly walked away and went on with my life.

For a while, this was a recurring scenario in my life. Even long-time friends got physical or tried to intimidate me when I refused drugs and alcohol from them. This was heartbreaking having close friends turn on me because I didn't want their drugs. My last drink was on my thirtieth birthday. A friend bought me a bourbon and coke, and after one sip I knew did not want to drink anymore. My senses dulled, I could not hold a thought or intelligent conversation, and I felt like the empty version of the self I had once been. I washed the drink down with glass after glass of water and plenty of food. It wasn't very pleasant, and I couldn't wait for it to be over.

Just for some food for thought: I'd like to just shed some light on some statistics that are associated with drinking alcohol. (Numbers in a section like this are fine!)

www.aihw.gov.au states that 1 in 6 people drink at levels that place them at risk of an alcohol related disease.

www.pubs.niaaa.nih.gov shows that the following violent crimes committed, were all committed under the influence of alcohol:

- 86% of homicide offenders

- 60% of sexual offenders

- 57% of men & 27% of women in marital violence

- 13% of child abusers

All these numbers are suspected to be much higher due to the lack of testing provided.

I am aware that this may be a shock to some people, and there are many other dangers that come from consuming alcohol, but I do feel that many of those things get enough airtime, such as car accidents, health issues, and addiction. By reducing the amount of alcohol you have, you are making the world a better place. For me personally, as I mentioned previously, I would not have done half the destructive things in my life, had it not been for the consumption of too much alcohol.

Alcohol seems to be the most common trap in society today, along with gambling. Because it is socially acceptable to have a drink, even encouraged, no one sees the harm it brings with it. I have personally witnessed family breakdown and dysfunction in my own family and in many others around me as a result of alcohol. It is one of the most heartbreaking things to see close friends lose everything because they are controlled by the urge to take drugs or get drunk. I have witnessed the relentless abuse and the tears that come in the aftermath of mixing trauma and bad coping mechanisms.

I offer you this challenge: take one month off alcohol, gambling, and/or drugs you may take. It's just thirty days. Take note of those who support your decision, and those who want to sabotage you. Those who hinder you - keep them at arm's length. Those who support you and wish you well – keep them close, as these are the people who really love you and wish to see you succeed. People who don't want to share and celebrate your victories, do not give them the time of day. Save your breath for those who care for you.

CHAPTER 6

RESPONSIBILITY

> "It really doesn't matter whose fault it is that something
> is broken
> It's your responsibility to fix it
> " **Will Smith**

Suck it up.

I understand this will ruffle the feathers of those who are not ready to hear this, but for others, this may be the push that is needed. One of the hardest obstacles I have faced in my life was an undiagnosed case of post-traumatic stress disorder. I thought I had lost my mind every waking moment of the day. I would daydream of outlaw motorbike clubs hunting me down and underworld figures offering me safety for the price of my soul. Little did anyone know I was reliving the horrors of my past. I was quickly written off by healthcare professionals as a patient with either psychosis or schizophrenia. So, every day, I was medicated with a cocktail of drugs, some of which are very dangerous if not administered properly. I could sit here and blame the medical staff for diagnosing me incorrectly, or I could understand that maybe I was to blame for this. How could I be to blame for their negligence? Quite simply put, I did not share the relevant information of my past, and I didn't believe they would understand what I had been through.

Whilst I took the wrong medications for a mental health issue I didn't have, I also self-medicated and had done so for many years. Honestly, if I hadn't numbed the painful thoughts and emotions, maybe I would have dealt with my problems a whole lot better. I could very easily blame medical professionals for not doing their job properly, but if I looked after myself properly and avoided the temptations of drugs and alcohol, it's very likely I would not have been in the situation to begin with.

After close to ten years of mental health issues and medication that made feel like a zombie, I decided not to take anymore medication. Instead, I tried to talk about my problems. I would stay up all night learning NLP (Neurolinguistic programming) techniques to gain control of my mind and learn how to deal with destructive thoughts, depression, and anxiety. Although my psychologist was good at his job, I did not feel as though I was making progress.

So, I decided to go to university and study behavioural science to try and understand the human condition and how to bring about the change I so desperately wanted. Not long after I started, however, I was sentenced to prison for the assault I previously mentioned. My journey did not end there, though. At first, I was mad at what this man had done that sent me to prison, and I sought revenge regularly. But, as time passed, that anger and hatred would turn to gratitude.

In prison I began working out every day, several times a day. I gave up my cigarette habit of over fifteen years. This would go on to be the catalyst of change that took me from living in an alcohol-fuelled place I called home, to where I am today. During my time in jail, I suffered from the pain of my past which was exacerbated by the types of people around me. After my release, I began to aim for a new life. I soon discovered that I would not find this life at my mum's house, as she was fighting her own demons. I would not find it a thousand kilometres away, at my best friend's house, as he had his own life to live and his own struggles to face. I would find it looking in the mirror of my beat-up old Holden Commodore, where I slept most nights, driving from beach to beach and car park to car park. Those lonely nights fuelled my anger and fed the demons of my soul, stirring up more hatred against those who had wronged me. Why was I here? How come I have no one? And why do I even bother? I looked at groups of people around me, friends and family, boyfriends and girlfriends. I then looked at myself; why, was all I could ask.

I continued to work out every day, running up to ten kilometres a day and doing push ups, sit ups, and squats until I was tired enough to rest. As night grew closer, I would look for a beach, because at the beach I would generally find a cold shower beach goers used to wash off. Every day I would have my cold shower and brush my teeth, always worrying about staying in one place for too long, in case people noticed I was homeless.

I soon realised I had to socialise for my own sanity. I would go days without speaking to anyone, and sometimes I would be sitting thinking, "Have I spoken today?" I couldn't just sit down and wait for people to speak to me, so I would go window shopping and speak to cashiers and customers, tacitly alluding to my circumstances. Instead of saying I was actually homeless, I would say, "I live just down there" and vaguely gesture towards the beach. Or, if I stumbled upon some backpacking tourists, I would say that I was doing some travelling around Australia as well. More often than not, they would invite me round to spend the evening with them.

So, I was taking care of myself as well as I could: exercise, hygiene, and socialising were taken care of. I was living on the bare minimum when it came to food as money was sometimes quite scarce, even though I had sold many of my possessions. I learned to make three-dollar pasta, which would feed a small family. I would buy a $1 can of tuna, $1 packet of pasta, and a $1 pasta sauce or can of tomatoes. I cooked the pasta on a small camping stove I stored in my car, and once cooked, I put it in a pan with the tuna and sauce, mixed it all in and heated it through, and *voila*. I would conjure up many little dishes like this and try to look after myself as best as I could. I soon learned that no matter where you are in Australia, somewhere some shop will have a multivitamin on sale for half price. If I had the money and the opportunity presented itself, I would purchase one and take it daily, to make up for anything I was lacking.

One day, after giving up alcohol, I was sitting by the water and realised that if I was to have any shot at a future and have peace of mind free of the torment my mind delivered to me daily, I would have to get some help - psychological help. On days when I struggled more than others, I would try to call one of the helplines that come up when you type 'suicide' into Google. It concerns me that many of them were all but useless. I would try to openly discuss my problems, only to encounter a counsellor with a flowchart script, "So you're feeling like this. Have you tried this?" I learned in my early years that a good counsellor offers very little to no advice because the client already knows what has to be done. They just need to talk about what ails them, so that they can get some clarity and move forward. Other times, I was met with obnoxious people who seemed like they had had enough and didn't even care. On one occasion I encountered a female counsellor, who clearly had it in for males and was ready to tear you down for being a male.

Fortunately, I found one helpline to be more helpful then all the rest - the kid's helpline. Even though I was twenty-two-years-old, they have a cut off age of twenty-five, so I just made the cut. The best thing about this helpline was I that was able to talk to the same counselor each time and didn't have to repeat my story. I began to openly talk to this man about what was happening in my life and how I was feeling. I told him about the loneliness that plagued me and the past that kept me up at night and was there to greet me in the morning. All of a sudden, I didn't feel like "an outcast", or "a loser". I was just a decent guy who was down on his luck. I started believing in myself and even started writing poetry again, facing all the fears and darkness, baring my soul.

Before long, I joined a homeless refuge, and to the surprise of all the program directors and youth workers, I proved to be someone who just might beat the cycle of homelessness and poverty. Here I was, twenty-three years old, working out daily, was sober, no longer doing drugs or smoking cigarettes. I also set out to help those in need and began volunteering at the homeless kitchen and doing a course in community service. I would also go on to gain employment where I was promptly promoted. I joined a martial arts gym, where I could continue to exercise and let out any and all of my frustrations. I chose to start seeing a psychologist with whom I openly shared the stories of being involved in crime and the reasons I was still scared that some bad people may still be after me. I also began to talk about the trouble I had faced at home, things I had never told anyone. To my surprise, the psychologist said that I was NOT suffering from schizophrenia, but rather an anxiety disorder named PTSD.

I was given the appropriate medication, fluoxetine, or Prozac as it is commonly known, a very common SSRI that, within hours, gave me the mental stability I had only dreamt of. And just like that, my mind was mine again, and I was finally talking about everything I had held in for so long. I always thought that if I shared my thoughts, it would get people in trouble. But in this case the only person who really had to deal with the trouble was me.

Many things in life are easy to blame on others, but was it the previous health practitioner's fault they gave me a wrong diagnosis and medication, or was it mine for not sharing the appropriate information? Was I self-medicating, mistakenly trying to do everything I could to keep my mental health in check and then expecting the health care system to fix me when I was not even going to stop the daily self-medication? Even though taking the new medication helped things improve, this is not the only thing that contributed to the recovery of my mental health. I had to take responsibility for every area of my life and do what I could with what I had.

I had no gym membership, so I worked out on the beach; I had no home or place to shower, so I used the cold public showers; I wasn't getting enough nutrition, so I found a cheap way to supplement; I had no one to talk to, so I would talk to cashiers and random people on the street. It was no one's responsibility but my own to pick myself up and get myself to a place where I could be a functioning member of society. Looking back, I have nothing but love and gratitude for those who wronged me. Without those people and experiences, I would not have learnt the lessons and the skills I have today that picked me up off the streets, got me off drugs and alcohol, and made me respect myself to the degree I do today.

So, to all the people who I assumed put me in jail, beat the crap out of me, introduced me to drugs and alcohol, and made my life harder than it ever had to be, I am sorry I ever held you responsible for things I could have done something about.

My challenge to you, the reader, is to look at the things you blame others for and ask yourself, "If I took responsibility for this, what would it look like?"

CHAPTER 7

CLEAN HOME

"The space in which we live should be for the person we
are becoming now,
not for the person we were in the past."
Marie Kondo

There is an amazing movie that was later made into a series called *Limitless*. A brief overview of this show is: a down and out writer is battling to keep his head above water. His girlfriend leaves him, and his publicist wants to drop him as he has become an alcoholic. Just as it looks like nothing can go right to pull him out this slump, he is approached by his dead-beat brother in-law who has now miraculously got his life together. His brother-in-law offers him what is quite literally a magic pill, promising that it will solve all his problems and get his life back on track. The writer accepts saying, what the hell, I've got nothing else to lose.

Now, I am not advocating that a magic pill will magically solve all your problems, but I can guarantee you will be in a much better place if you implement some of the practices in this book. The first thing the provocateur does after taking this pill that unlocks his mind's potential, is to quite simply clean his house. Walking into his home he is astounded and exclaims, "Is this where I live?" So, the very first thing he decides to do with limitless potential is clean up his home. Once his home is in perfect order, only then does he attempt to work on his book, which is long overdue.

"You're so O.C.D." "You're a neat freak!" These are common phrases or lighthearted insults I grew up with, as if to say if you are a tidy person, you must have something wrong with you. It was always associated with being somewhat neurotic. I never considered myself neurotic, but I was always a very organised person. My mind always felt cluttered when things were a mess. So, instead of ignoring the problem, I just cleaned it up and made my living space somewhat pleasant. I never realised the implications of these habits until later in life when I sat and discussed topics such as depression, anxiety, and social work with a friend, who had been working in this field for many years. This wise, unassuming man stood just above my shoulder height, had a razored bald head with a long beard and if you didn't know him you would think he was a scary sort of person. Although covered in tattoos and standing staunch as a large tree trunk, he was one of the nicest people I had ever met. This gem of a man went by the name of Ray. I still remember the gem he dropped on me one day as he reflected on his career in social work. He said, "I could always tell if someone was suffering from depression the moment I walked into their house."

As Ray and I discussed this correlation between a clean home and mental health, I painted mental images of homes I had been in throughout my life. Many of these homes were in low-income areas. They were generally extremely messy throughout. One house even had small goat tracks among the hoarded trash one had to wade through to get from one room to another. Surely, the relationship between low-income homes and cleanliness is not the reason many people find it hard to leave these poverty-stricken areas and lifestyles. Truth be told, I don't know, but I am sure the added stress that comes from a messy home cannot help the already stressful life of overdue rent and utility bills, food and clothing and everything else life tends to hand us when we are down-and-out. As a first step though, a free one at that, we can tidy up our homes and begin to bring some order into our already chaotic existence. I understand the relationship between being a tidy person and individual personality traits is closely linked, so it may not be that important to you and you may not see the benefit at all, and that's okay. I do ask though, what do you have to lose?

As I sit here, I find it hard to imagine letting my home get messier and messier with each passing day. I have never even considered what my life would be like if I never cared about the state of my home. I sometimes use the gem that Ray dropped all those years ago as a gauge of mental health. I look around the house and ask: is the rubbish taken out? Are the clothes washed? What have I been neglecting? And generally, if my home begins to resemble a pigsty, I know I have to take some time to get my house in order, or I may quite possibly become overburdened with stress.

People have written many books about the importance of keeping a clean home or making your bed, and the benefits associated with these things. My advice is - start small. Start with the easiest task first and go from there. Being more organised at home is a skill that, once mastered, expresses itself in other areas of life. You will perform better at work, find more time for your partner and/or kids, and with a bit of luck, even find time for yourself. As far as skills go in the people I would consider employing, first trait on my list is whether or not the person is conscientious or not. When I am looking at people to work with, I don't really care about qualifications or how creative they are; I need them to be able to organise themselves so that productivity is the inevitable outcome.

Sit with this thought for a while. Imagine you have an assistant, and you ask them to find the number of someone you wish to contact. As they begin to search through piles of paperwork, their phone, and every other place it could be, to no avail, how do you feel? Frustrated, right? You are faced with an incompetent assistant who, instead of bringing you solutions and results, is creating more problems for you. After this frustrating situation has played out, you are more inclined to resent your assistant for their behaviour. Does that sound about right?

Now, here is the kick in the pants - not only is this person making your life harder, but this person is you if you can't keep a clean and tidy home. You ultimately have the power to make your life as easy or as hard as it needs to be. How can you expect someone to do things for you when you lack the skills to do things for yourself. It is easy to find fault in assistants who we pay to serve us and blame their shortcomings for making our lives more difficult, but what if we held ourselves to the same standard we hold them?

This chapter may seem more about becoming more organised generally than actually about cleaning your house, but the two go hand in hand. You cannot maintain an organised life when your home and lifestyle is a mess.

As Jordan Peterson says, "Go clean your room"

CHAPTER 8

LISTEN

"God gave us two ears and one mouth
so we should listen twice as much as we speak"
Tupac Shakur

We all of have that one friend, or maybe a few, who are so eager to tell you the intricate details of their lives, the ups, the downs, the things they regret, the things they are excited for in the future. That one friend who won't shut up ... and when it is your turn to talk or add an opinion, you are cut off and forced to hear more from that person. So, you inevitably don't get one word in. Although this friend may be a good person with good intentions, at some point talking to this person becomes more of a burden than a blessing and you can find yourself beginning to resentment them. "Why does this person never listen to me?". This is a very toxic relationship, and until we learn to adopt the old adage of "do not cast your pearls before swine", we will be doomed to repeat this over and over again.

Hurling empty threats, my breath tainted with the smell of alcohol, I slammed the phone down - me and my best friend Sabastian, whom I consider to be somewhat of a brother to me, started our friendship on a rocky start. I never thought I would be face to face with the voice on the other end of that call.

Time went by and I had long forgotten about the phone call when I visited a friend's home and sitting on the couch, was a short, stocky Italian man, glaring at me.

I introduced myself and shook Sebastian's hand.

He replied with, "You don't remember me, do you?"

"No, should I?" I enquired.

As fate would have it, this was the man I had hurled threats at over the phone. Fortunately, he was a kind and understanding man and we agreed to leave the incident in the past.

I began to hang out with Sebastian more regularly, and found him to be a decent person to be around. Although I had numerous friends at the time, I still felt invisible and disrespected. After getting to know Sebastian, I felt comfortable talking to him and to my surprise he would be quiet and listen intently, as if what I had to say was somewhat important and worth listening to. Whether it was me sharing some sorrow or a win I had had, it was never overshadowed by a sorrow he had had in the past, or how his wins were more important. Unfamiliar with this, I grew suspicious. "Why is he nice to me?" "What's his game?" "He must be up to something."

Years of mistrust followed; it was if I was chasing a unicorn. Every time I did not understand his motives or actions, I would say, "that's not right", and my anxiety would amplify any and all reasons to not trust him. Why would someone be this nice to me? I was so accustomed to people acting in their own self-interests and being left high-and-dry and all alone, that I could not fathom what a healthy relationship was.

A few years down the line, I began to question everyone I considered close friends and family. Are these people really my friends, and are they worth my time? So, I tried an experiment: who would call me if I stopped calling or messaging them? And just like that, eighty percent of my "close friends" were gone. Shock would be a simple way of describing the way I felt. People I had known for years just disappeared off the face of the planet, as if they never existed. The disappointment didn't stop there either. The pain of isolation only sunk in deeper as time went by, leaving a sour taste in my mouth. "These people never gave a fuck about me." I was infuriated.

At least, I had the remaining twenty percent of my close companions. "I really should be grateful for that?"

Surprisingly, my phone rang one day, and I answered excitedly, happy to hear from one of my friends.

"Hey, man!" I said promptly. "Been a while?"

He responded with pleasantries, sharing the highs of his life—but then explained how things had recently taken a turn. They were now short on money, and he needed my help.

"My help?" I thought. I hadn't heard from this friend in years. Now, after all this time he calls me up to ask for some money because his addictions, both drugs and gambling, had gotten the better of him. "Was I the first person he called?" Of course, not. Being altruistic and basically kind at heart, I was dismayed that I had to decline to help him.

This phone call was an eyeopener because after that, the calls came rolling in, one after the other and all with a similar tone. "Hey, man, long time..." "So, I need to borrow some money." Same conversations with different people. They soon got the hint that I was not a loan shark and was not going to bail them out of their financial troubles.

Yet, like clockwork over the years, every other day, or once a week, my phone would ring - incoming call, Sebastian....

He never asked me for money or some favour. He would simply say to me, "Hey, man, how are you going?" A breath of fresh air. Seb called me regularly over the years, and I noticed he simply called to see how I was going and wondered what I had been up to. I would reciprocate with the same courtesy.

> *"A friend is someone you can share bad news with, and they will listen and share in your sorrow, but more importantly, a friend is someone you can share good news with, and they will celebrate with you." (Jordan B. Peterson)*

CHAPTER 9

HONESTY

"Honesty is the best policy."
Abraham Lincoln

"Just be yourself..."

Those are the infamous words of the Genie from the 90's Disney hit, *Aladdin*. Aladdin struggles with telling the princess he falls in love with the truth of where he comes from. "Street rat" is the label that plagues him as the woman he adores is presented with suitors that are quite literally royalty. Why would a princess want anything to do with a young homeless boy? What does he have to offer?

In my early twenties I was living a lonely existence by the beach. It was just me, my thoughts, and thankfully, a counsellor on the other end of the phone working a crisis line I called regularly to stop my mind from sinking into dark fear and sadness. Each morning, I woke up in the back seat of my run-down old car that I had paid way too much for, to be greeted by the day. One day I came across a thirty-five-year-old woman who was a tourist backpacker exploring Australia. She seemed nice enough and was open to the idea of hanging out and getting to know one another. As time went on, questions arose such as, "Where do you live?" to which I replied with a well-rehearsed and prompt answer, "just down there", ambiguously pointing in the general direction of the beach. I kept our get-togethers brief so as not to let on that I lived in my car and had no one around like friends or family.

One day, on a bush walk, she asked me a question that baffled me. "Are you one of those rich guys who pretends to be poor?" Stunned, I replied with a nervous, "No, sorry, not me", trying to shrug off the feeling of imminent rejection. Ours was nothing more than a platonic relationship and, as it happened, we never spoke again after that day. My worst fears were realised. Why would a girl want to be with me if I was nothing but a "Street Rat"? I managed to maintain what I believed to be an aura of wealth and health, a facade that helped people like me not give up their past or present.

Regardless of who I met, I re-framed my situation and fabricated a lie; I wasn't homeless, I was travelling, I wasn't lonely, I was finding myself. I guess no matter how you frame a turd, it is still a turd. Slowly, I settled down in my hometown with the help of local community services, such as Coast Shelter, a homeless charity. I found in some cases I could be honest with myself and others, but in others I maintained this hyper-confident persona. But I found a lot of people didn't like this persona. I met with a psychologist once or twice a month and discussed my pain with brutal honesty, like never before. Disappointingly, I started noticing that the relationship between me and the psychologist was developing into an inappropriate relationship, and I would have to end it. So, plagued by loneliness, I asked my final question, "Why don't people like me?" She left me with a generic answer, "With some people you give too much, and with others you don't give enough". I struggled at this answer, as it only raised more questions.

I began to look more carefully at the people I was trying to include in my life, and asked myself, "What do these people even have to offer?" I noticed that maybe it wasn't me who was the problem. I took inventory of my life: "I don't drink, smoke, or do drugs." "I am an honest person who goes above and beyond for people I choose to help," and so on. The list goes on. Then I looked at the people around me… I noticed that I brought more value to each of their lives than they did to mine. In too many cases, the people in question did more harm than good and were more willing to take than to give. So maybe, just maybe, I was not the problem. I had worked so hard to be to others the man I wish I had had growing up to guide me. Consequently, I was surrounded by people who didn't really care at all about me and my well being. The question I should have asked the psychologist was not, "Why don't people like me?" but "How do I find more like-minded people to surround myself with?"

I started putting down roots in different surroundings where I could mix with a higher class of person. Please note that when I say higher class I do not necessarily mean people's financial position or status. I mean their good morals and values; people whose character is a beacon of light. I began to share and be honest in the public sphere, as my stories were somewhat motivational and inspiring. I took up poetry and began performing in front of large groups of people, baring my soul, my story and the truth, with complete strangers, who listened without judgement or censure. I gained a confidence I had never experienced before. I could be myself, and nothing bad would happen. Even if it did, I was ready for the challenge. I slept easy each night, knowing I could bare my soul to the world and be uplifted and encouraged.

Yet feelings of inadequacy lurked behind doors and crept out in moments of weakness. Sometimes, I would meet a nice girl from the good side of town who had no idea how hard life could be, and I would slip back into that false persona with my hidden shame. The same would go with high status men I wished to impress or work with in the future.

This was the moment I found the correlation between myself and Aladdin - I met a girl who seemed interested in me. She was from the right side of the tracks, a part of town that hadn't even seen train tracks, and I felt like, "if this girl knew the truth, she wouldn't want to be with me." So, after a short time getting to know her, I couldn't shake this feeling. I consulted a close friend, who was a few years ahead of me and whom I admired deeply. I asked Mr Riley, "What should I do?" and as the genie suggested in the Disney movie, he tells me to be myself ... if she can't accept that, she's probably not the one for you. He went on to say that people admire a man who comes from nothing; it can be a strength that helps your journey rather than hinders it.

So, little by little, I opened up to this girl. After one week and not that much sharing, if I am honest, the phone stopped ringing.

As much as it sucks to be on the receiving end of rejection, it was the right thing to have happened. If we had kept hanging out, would her feelings ever have faded? Was it more a reflection of what she actually thought of me? I had not felt that shameful about my past in such a long time.

Some time passed and I put dating on the back burner. I threw myself into my work, health, and well-being and decided not to focus on girls. I started *All That Entertainment*; a company aimed at developing creative artists and provide opportunities for people I believed in. I began to take my martial arts even more seriously and began coaching Mixed Martial Arts, or MMA, and would go on to publish an instructional book.

Then, as a kind twist of fate, I met a beautiful woman, one that by all rights should have made me feel so small and unworthy, a literal "Street Rat", and yet she didn't...

We began talking over messages and phone calls; some phone calls lasted into the early hours of the morning. I remember looking at my phone in disbelief one day—a six-hour phone call! This amazing woman was from India. She was very fit and healthy, didn't drink or do drugs, worked out, and had a high-paying corporate job. This alone struck me as WOW. She was a quality person who cared about herself, and I would go on to discover she cared for others too. On our late-night walks, she would see a homeless man on the side of the footpath begging for food and, without any prompting from me, would take me into a store to buy a coffee and sandwich to give to the suffering man.

I began to learn more and more about this Indian princess. Like, for instance, she had a brief stint in modelling and was Miss South India, had the voice of an angel, and was doing her PhD in Economics. The more she shared with me, the more I should have cowed away behind my persona, yet I didn't. I opened up, was brutally honest with her, and confessed to feeling like Aladdin in the Disney movie! However, the difference here was I did not feel like I had to pretend to be a prince for her to like me. So, when she looked up at me as we watched a movie together and asked, "Will you be my boyfriend?" I was shocked, but of course replied with a definite, "Yes".

The right person can make you feel like a king even when you feel more like a bum. I genuinely feel like I met a princess, skipped the part where I had to pretend to be someone else and went straight into an open, honest relationship with not only her, but myself as well.

People will not always like you or reciprocate the kindness you show them, but that doesn't always mean that something is wrong with you. Maybe you are simply birds of a different feather, and it's time to fly from the nest and move forward with your life. Life is complicated enough, so when we hide from others and ourselves behind a persona of who we think people will accept, we may be robbing ourselves of a great future and great experiences. If you truly believe you are doing everything you can to be a better person, then it really doesn't matter what others think or have to say about your life. Find people who love you regardless of your mistakes and shortcomings. Find people who wish to see you grow and flourish even when you're down and out.

The hardest thing for me to overcome was to begin to be honest with myself, but when I did, life began to work *for* me and not happen *to* me. And I am sure it will for you as well.

CHAPTER 10

"CHALLENGE ACCEPTED"

"You gain strength, courage, and confidence by every experience in which you really stop to look fear in the face"
Eleanor Roosevelt

Barney Stinson from the hit TV show *How I Met Your Mother*, played by Neil Patrick Harris, had a catch phrase that was so deep and profound you may have missed the importance of it due to the humour which usually followed. This catch phrase was "Legen... Wait for it... dary! Legendary!" I joke; it was "Challenge accepted". Faced with the odds stacked against him, Barney Stinson would accept the challenge he was presented with every time, no matter how stupid it seemed.

So, in this chapter we are going to look at how, twice in my life, this mentality pulled me out of the darkest periods of my life.

PART ONE

To start, we go back to a time before I was diagnosed with PTSD. I lived with my symptoms, day-in, day-out, in what seemed like dark abyss from the moment I opened my eyes, every day. Now, when I say every day, I do mean every day. The demons of my past haunted me on a daily basis. Like clockwork I would wake up in the morning, and for 10 to

15 seconds my mind was at ease. Then, the shadows of my past would sneak in and torment my mind, many times pushing me to the brink of suicide, or at the very least an escape into alcohol. This was a real problem for me, day-in, day-out. At least when I closed my eyes, I had peace in my dreams. Until I mentioned this to someone, and wished I hadn't; that night, the nightmares that usually only lurked through the daylight hours, crept into my dreams as well. So, now I suffered 24 hours of hell ... day-in, day-out.

At this point in my life I had given up on the medication that had made me feel like a zombie, which in hindsight was the wrong medication, and had begun to talk to a psychologist on a semi regular basis. In all honesty though, despite the fact that I spoke to him frequently, I told him nothing. I chose my words extremely carefully, scared that I would be judged and labelled a crazy person. This was a poor decision because I would have to start being completely open and honest to begin my road to recovery. I was taking the steps in the right direction; I was educating myself on-line, learning coping mechanisms and strategies, using tools from NLP (Neurolinguistic programming), and even enrolling in a university to learn behavioural studies—anything I could, but to no avail. I would remain a prisoner to my mind, to my past, and to destructive thoughts.

One sleepless night, I came across an online forum that asked: Are you a chump or a champ? It explained how the stories we tell ourselves shape our future, and in a fill-in-the-blanks style format, it asked me to retell my life as a chump, then to go back and do it again with the mindset of a champ. This was a huge moment in my life. It was a turning point that would begin to shape the man I became. Somewhere in the text of this on-line exercise was a kick-in-the-pants that said: When faced with adversity from the past, the present. or the future. you have three options. You can do nothing, and life will just happen to you. You can run away and try to escape it, or you can say "challenge accepted", and at least try to overcome it.

I want to be very clear about this though - when you begin saying "challenge accepted" to life's adversities, it is not a magic word that solves every problem. What it does do, however, is put you in the correct mindset to face the your problems.

So, that night I made a decision: I knew I was going to struggle when I woke up in the morning, but instead of rolling over and accepting my fate as I had done for years, I was going to adopt a mantra and a mindset of "challenge accepted". When I opened my eyes the next morning, the first thing I said was just that: "Challenge accepted." My challenge was an obstacle I could do nothing about, but with this new mindset it began to seem like maybe, just maybe, it didn't have to be as bad. So, although my destructive thoughts still plagued my mind and the fears of the past still owned a lot of real estate in my brain each day, my mood lifted a little. I felt like, although I was suffering, I was going to be okay. I would get through this eventually.

I would love to tell you this solved everything, and I never suffered again, but this is definitely not the case. What it did do was pick me up and begin to build a foundation for what would become an amazing recovery. As they say, Rome was not built in a day, and neither will your mental health. It takes time, good life decisions, a strong social network, sometime professional and/or medical intervention. These are all small parts of a whole that will help you.

PART TWO

Before I met my beautiful wife, I was in a long-term relationship for almost five years. In hindsight, it wasn't the healthiest relationship, but we persevered nonetheless. At this point in our relationship, we had her mother living with us, two dogs, and even a guinea pig, so the house was quite stressful. The week of our five-year anniversary, I was sitting on the couch playing a video game, taking some time to relax, when my ex approached me and asked to talk. I paused the game and asked, "Of course.

What's up?" With a degree of hesitation in her voice, she blurted out, "I don't want to marry you, I don't want to have kids with you." Shocked, I replied, "Okay. Why? What's up."

She went on to say she loved me, but more like a brother. She then proposed a solution which, to me, was a shocking compromise I could not accept. She wanted us stay together, but we could also see other people. I immediately answered with a hard no. I was definitely not okay with this arrangement, as someone would get hurt emotionally and, if I found someone in my bed, possibly physically as well. I asked her to consider whether or not this was what she really wanted, and to get back to me. The following day, after getting no answer from her, I approached her and said, "It seems as if you have made your decision."

I would go on to leave her and her mother, the house with everything in it, and take only my TV, play station, my car, and the clothes on my back.

I was lucky enough at the time to have a friend who had a room for rent, at least for a short period of time. After picking up my entire life and starting again, I was in a deep depression, one that would lead me back to suicidal ideology. If my life can come crashing down after all the hard work I had put in, why was it worth it anymore? To top things off, the place I had just moved into was now being vacated, and I had nowhere else to go. I thought to myself, "I guess I am homeless again... FANTASTIC" Feeling like giving up, I drove around in my car with a length of rope tied and twisted into a last resort - a hangman's noose.

Before moving out, I was sitting on the bed that came with the house, pondering and crying and fearing for my future. I began to remember the mindset that had helped me so much before, and thought to myself, "CHALLENGE ACCEPTED." Just like that, my thoughts shifted from the chump I was being: "I am homeless and worthless", to the champ mindset of: "How does this work in my favour?" So, I began to think of possible solutions. I began to think about how I would manage life. I started with: I guess I can live in my car again, but where will I shower? ... probably at the beach or something. This was the logical first step for me.

Trying to problem-solve, I began to think about websites and apps like flat-finder and other matchmaker businesses that provide affordable housing. At this point I was still thinking like a chump, "why would anybody want to live with me?" That is, until those thoughts were replaced with ones of my inner champ that said, "Nah, man, challenge accepted." It wasn't me who was lucky to find a room to rent, it was the person looking for someone to rent their room who would be lucky to find me. I began to realise my worth and think about the positive qualities that I possess that made me a prime candidate - I am a very tidy person. I don't drink, smoke, or do drugs, which means less dramas. I spend a lot of time working, and when I get home, I just want to spend time with myself, which means I stayed out of everyone's hair, and the list began to grow. I began applying for rooms and found several. Each home I visited, I noticed very quickly I was a rare commodity in the house-share market. Now I got to choose who I stayed with and not so much who wanted me to stay.

I chose an older man who ran his own business and was very tidy. We got along like a house on fire, ripping on each other due to him being from England and myself from Australia. Things just began to work out for me again. I was ready to face the world again.

This mantra has changed my life in more ways than I can describe and continues to do so, not only for me but also for others who choose to adopt this way of life for themselves. During workouts, when I am not feeling too hot and I don't really want to be there, I just say, "challenge accepted."

During times that are unproductive, look within and accept the challenge. Not only will you grow more courageous, but you will also do things you never thought possible. You will be able to recreate yourself in ways that make you unrecognisable as months go by. You won't always beat the challenges ahead of you. Don't let this discourage you and your growth. Each time you are confronted with something difficult, this champ mindset will help you get better and give you a way to grow and move forward.

As a personal challenge I want you to go and face something you thought you couldn't. Whether it's your thoughts first thing in the morning, or something in your relationships at home or work. Begin facing these challenges instead of shying away from them. If I can do it, so can you. The only difference between you and me is that I've given you a head start by showing you the power of this mindset. You don't have to work it out yourself.

CHAPTER 11

BE A GOOD PERSON

BECAUSE NO ONE WANTS TO WORK WITH A DICKHEAD

> "Those who are happiest are those who do the most for others."
> **Booker T. Washington**

I was a juvenile delinquent and a self-proclaimed menace to society when I was a teenager. I would constantly find myself getting into mischief, sometimes warranting a visit from local law enforcement. My criminal activities started small, as most people who take this path find out. It starts with hanging out with some new friends, and one day you decide to try and steal a chocolate from the local corner store or service station.

Picture this: three young boys dressed in hand-me-downs enter the store, hearts beating so hard and fast that even the store clerk can hear the beating drums. With a watchful eye, the clerk follows us around the store and enquires, "Can I help you?" "No," we reply nonchalantly, "We're just looking". We then split up, as the clerk cannot be in three places at once. I reach for my favourite bubbly mint chocolate on the shelf, my hands trembling with adrenaline and fear of being caught. I place it in the waistline of my pants, hidden from sight by my oversized T-shirt. Looking around to try and spot the clerk, I see he is somewhere else. I turn for the door and, not knowing where my friends are, I sneak out. I take several steps and then run from the scene of the crime.

I had done it! The perfect crime.

From this point on, after seeing how easy it was to just take what I wanted, I did just that. I could steal cigarettes and sell them at school for a dollar apiece. I could take blocks of chocolate to school for lunch and have something to eat. As time went on, the ease of these minor crimes lost their spark, and I began taking more and more risks. I went from taking the hood ornaments of cars, to taking the whole car. We got caught after this and I was brought into the police station along with my new friends and, thankfully, let off with a warning. This was how most people in our community lived, so I could not for the life of me understand why bad things kept happening to me. After all, I was probably one of the better-behaved boys in our group of wannabe thugs. To me, a lifestyle of crime, drugs and alcohol, and violence was just how life was lived. It was normal. I didn't know I had a choice. Later on, not understanding that choices have consequences, it would baffle me how I got to the point where I had to sleep on the street, or at best, on a friend's couch.

I never knew anyone who had a full-time job and lived the so-called American Dream. To me, this was a Hollywood concoction. No one actually had a happy family, owned their own home, and so on and so forth. I believed most people were like me and grew up around drugs, crime, and violence. To me, this was life.

I had a true wake-up call one day. Many people had warned me to walk away from this life as I was going to get serious real soon as the threat of outlaw motorcycle clubs was inevitable. They were right.

As I cowered behind a dumpster, hiding and praying for my safety, the five or six friends I was with scattered as cars pulled up from every direction. Young men began running out from behind a building. At the time, it seemed as if one hundred people were running in our direction, fully intending to inflict as much harm as possible. Yelling and screaming filled the air and the large bin I was hidden behind was pushed up against a fence, and I was surrounded. A young man dressed in black jumped on top of the bin, searching for me and my friends. In this moment, I said a prayer, "God, I don't know if you're real, but if you are, I need your help. If you can get me out of this alive and unscathed, I will walk away from this life forever." I went on to say, knowing full well I had never known any other life, "I will need your help because I have no idea how to do that."

After I finished this prayer, the young man dressed in black looked down at me, and another man came around the side of the bin and went to pull me out, only to be stopped by the first man. He said to him, "Leave him. He's okay." With a quiet whisper, he tells me, "Wait here until we are all gone."

Several days before this encounter, I had met this young man dressed in black and he was, in fact, the man who gave me the warning to walk away from this life I was pursuing. If it had been any other man on the top of that bin, I would have ended up like my friend that night – with my mouth booted in and some missing teeth, at the very least.

Naively, I continued to go down the same path over and over, never learning my lesson. I went on to hold some young men hostage, in a drunken and drug-induced attempt to be what I thought was -The Man, only to have hardened criminals from an outlaw motorcycle club do the same to me and my best friend. We narrowly escaped what could have been a new pair of weighted shoes and a not-so-pleasant swim. Looking back now, I finally understand how you really do reap what you sow.

Several years later, alone, homeless and finally prepared to make something of myself, I began to aim to be a better person. I started small, by paying forward a pie at a bakery, so the following person would receive a free pie. This small practice made me feel like I was somebody worthwhile and gave me the warm fuzzy feelings I think I really needed, especially then. I began to lend a helping hand wherever I saw one was needed, whether it was an old lady on the side of the road with a flat tyre or someone who needed a hand moving a piece of furniture. I began to stop thinking about just myself and my own needs and instead considered the world around me and chose to be a servant to those in need.

I was faced with an internal dilemma though. I was giving the little I did have and helping people who had much more than me. Growing up, I had always despised with an aggressive jealousy those who were financially secure, yet here I was helping them.

After struggling with why I should continue to help people, I chose to continue, realising that although these people may not necessarily be suffering financially, they may be suffering from depression, anxiety, loneliness, relationships issues, and God knows what else. And if nothing else, it made someone's day, and they might go on and do the same for someone else. Not long after I started this life as a servant, I got some much-needed employment on a fishing boat, which gave me not only financial security but also a place to stay, as the gracious young skipper allowed me to live on the boat when we were in port. I remember to this day how, with my first paycheck, I dreamed of all the ways I could help others and where my unique skills would best be placed.

Sitting quietly one night in port on the swaying fishing boat, I contemplated my life and truly reflected on my decisions and all the things I had done wrong. I had stolen from friends and family, shops, and strangers. I had been a very violent person, hurting quite a few people with my anger, and much, much more. I decided to write down all the things I had done wrong, in point form. I knew I could not live with these burdens weighing heavy on my chest and writing them down was bringing them to light. I wanted resolution and peace of mind, so I began to look on-line for the people I had wronged. One by one, I contacted them, confessed the wrong I had done, and offered either compensation or resolution or both. Every conversation made my heart thump with fear and worry. There was no guarantee that anyone would forgive me, but I was committed to this.

I recall one conversation with a best friend from primary school. I had messaged him for the first time in many years.

"Hey, man, long time no see. I just wanted to clear the air on something."

He replied, "Hey, mate, what's up?"

I went on to tell him, back when we were kids, I was the one who had stolen his Pokémon game for his Game Boy. The irony was I did not even have a Game Boy to play it on. I offered to replace the old video game or give him the money for what it was worth today. As I waited, anxiously watching the chat screen's animated dots: TYPING ... his reply shocked me.

This old friend told me that he knew I had taken it, and that it was okay. He could not believe I was still worrying about this after all these years. He said he didn't want any compensation or anything. It was all good. After laughing about it together, I downloaded the game on my computer and for the first time in my life, played the Pokémon game with a clear conscience.

A year or two after this, I was living in a homeless refuge and finally putting the building blocks of my life together with this new philosophy of being a servant to my community and coming clean about my shortcomings. As a start, I volunteered in the homeless kitchen which, when I was a kid, had given my family free dinners and clothing. I would also go on to volunteer with another charity that mentored disadvantaged and vulnerable youth, and I helped raise money to support the charity's programs.

For once in my life, things just seemed to fall into place. I was offered jobs from everywhere, even at the places I was volunteering. I secured a house to rent and made many new friends. This was especially nice, as my old friends had not chosen the same path as me and found themselves frequenting jail, rehab, and mental health facilities. Many of them had no aspiration to be of significant value to the broader community, wishing instead for the downfall of those around them, even if only subconsciously.

The biggest moments of perspective came when I bumped into my past; people I had admired who had stayed on the same destructive path. I saw I no longer had things in common with them, and now the tables had turned. They now looked up to me and would tell me they were trying to turn their lives around. These conversations were repeated over and over, as if they had to prove themselves to me or somehow justify why they were still in the same life after all these years. A common excuse I heard was. "Yeah... but you were never as bad with (add in specific vice) as me", while at the same time being somewhat dismissive of the hard work I had put in to making a better life for myself. This shocked me, but I would shake it off, remembering the quote, "If you defend your weaknesses you get to keep them." I am not sure who said it, but it was very clear to me from the outside looking in.

The more I looked after my community and the people in it, the easier my life ultimately became. People offered me opportunities I would never even have dreamed of. I never thought my life would turn out the way it has. Whether or not you believe in karma, "you reap what you sew" or "what goes around, comes around", they all hold the same message: "just be a good person." And don't be fooled, this is no easy feat. It takes courage, sacrifice, and true humility.

As a personal challenge to you, I implore you to choose one time you wronged someone and go and make an amends with that person, face your shortcomings, and release yourself from the guilt of the past.

CHAPTER 12

ARE YOU READY TO RUMBLE

"Luck is what happens when preparation meets opportunity."
Seneca

The Covid 19 Pandemic was a crazy time for everyone.

The mandates and lock downs made things more and more difficult. Just before the lock downs began, I decided to leave my job and start an entertainment management company, *All That Entertainment*. At the time, I was positioned quite well to jump start my career. I had events and clients lined up and was booked out for the first six months. Days out from my first event, news feeds began to fill up about this virus that had been leaked from a lab in China. Cruise ships began docking in Australia, starting an outbreak an hour from where I live. Despite our best efforts, the event was cancelled - and as a cascading effect in the entertainment industry, everything was shut down. This left me with no work, picking up odd jobs here and there. To add insult to injury, my fiancé and I had just decided to have a child, and she was not long way from turning in her job to stay at home with the baby.

To make ends meet, I decided to start a handyman business, which blossomed into something that would sustain me and my new family. I began to think about the future and knew I wasn't going to be doing this for the rest of my life. But I would do what I had to for now. Nearly all the skill sets I have accumulated over the years were from experience, not from courses or books, but with the whole world in lock down, I needed to find another way to learn new skills. After a coffee with a friend, who had seen I was going through a tough time, he (or she) told me about an on-line education site, "Coursera", which offered a variety of on-line courses to up-skill. Many you could do for free. The course he recommended was the Science of Health and Well-Being from Yale University. I found the interface quite user friendly and pushed through the course. To my surprise, once I had finished, I found myself looking at other courses they offered. The next course that stood out was Business Negotiation. These courses had great integration between on-line learning and practical application. After this course, I would look at other courses, such as on-line marketing and advertising and any other thing I thought would help my entertainment company.

Using the new knowledge I had acquired, I systematised the lessons and integrated them into short workshop formats to provide a unique service to my clients. In doing so, I was bringing more value to the entertainment management and consulting I was doing and felt comfortable charging more for my services. I found all these skills transferred to other areas of my life, and I was learning to become a valuable asset to whichever organisation I was involved with. I was creating on-line content for the martial arts gym I had been training in for close to ten years, helping the owner reconsider ways he was handling business and trying to help the gym through the lock downs.

As the light appeared at the end of the tunnel and lock downs seemed to be coming to an end, we became excited. We could soon catch the train again, but to my surprise, our nation separated people into those who were vaccinated and those who were not. I had originally decided to get vaccinated but after being pressured and being told I had no choice; my natural instinct was to push back against the pressure. The ultimatum was presented - if you had the shot, you could go to gyms. If not, you were allowed to attend but would have to wait thirty days to return. Not a problem, I discussed my return after the thirty days with the owner, who was a mentor, a father figure, and my lead instructor. He was fine with it. However, to my surprise I received an email which informed me my membership had been cancelled. Shortly after that I see on Facebook that I was being replaced as the Mixed Martial Arts instructor. Oh, wow! I sometimes wonder what people in the future will think about this period in history. I fear we will look shameful indeed. Ten years of loyal service and support and not even a phone call or thank you.

Fast forward a few weeks, and my pregnant partner and I are at the petrol station getting fuel when I look over and see a bunch of young men with boxing hand wraps on, running as a team. I thought maybe they were a part of a gym close by, and to my surprise saw one across the road. I said to my partner that I wanted to go check it out soon. She agreed it was a good idea. A couple of days later, I went to get a haircut from my barber a few towns over, when a large Samoan man walked in wearing a T-shirt that had the gym's emblem on it. I introduced myself and asked about the gym and if he trained there. He laughed and said he, in fact, owned it. He began to tell me about the gym and its classes. I told him I would pop by to check it out. I mentioned I taught MMA, and he said he would love to have an MMA class one day.

Christmas was approaching, and he invited us to their gym's Christmas party and to bring the family. After meeting everyone, I decided I would go and try a class or two. The gym would close for a few weeks over Christmas, but I began training in January. By February I began teaching MMA. But what happened over the next few months would shake the very foundations of the gym. The owner's relationship with his partner broke down and coaches started leaving because they weren't being paid. People began leaving due to instability in the gym and coaches not showing up for classes. I had just started there, but because of my nature, I HAD to help and fill the hole in leadership and bring order to the chaos. So, by March, I appointed myself manager, as the owner had disappeared and no coaches were showing up. My first course of action was clean up, followed by showing up as coach to all of the classes, in case the other coaches didn't. Being a Mixed Martial Artist, I was qualified to teach all of the classes. Next, I proceeded to create a small shop, selling water and sports drinks, followed by training shorts and equipment. This helped me to employ another coach, who I could pay directly. This in turn took some weight off my shoulders.

For a few months, things began to work and the gym was finding its feet. In July, an opportunity arose to go to a two-day business seminar, which was headed by someone I really admired - David Balestri. I knew there was going to be some religious elements to the seminar. Not being "Christian", per se, I was okay with it because I understood the philosophical value that religion offered. The seminar was amazing. I learnt a lot and was learning new skills to bring more value to my business life and my personal life.

To my surprise, God spoke to me in those two days, breaking down all my questions and doubts until I had no choice but to surrender my pride and give my life to God. I realised the gym was where I was meant to be and felt God's hand guiding me to stay there. I was at a point in my journey with the gym that I was about to give up. I had been putting in the work for over seven months and doing everything in my power to keep the doors open. I applied all my skills that I had acquired over the years re-branding the gym with the same techniques and rules I had learned from my previous jobs, and skills I learned during lock down. I brought multiple streams of income into the gym and brought in clients and coaches to create the best gym I could for the owner.

But now, I had a change of heart. On the verge of burning out and throwing in the towel, I asked God how much longer I had to do this. I went on to say, "I feel like a fool, I have been working here for this long, not being paid, and the owner, full of empty promises, is really just lying to me." I felt God's presence, "Just a little longer." Okay, I thought.

At the seminar, we were taught that we own nothing, that we are just stewards for His kingdom, and we should aim to serve Him for His will to be done His way. So that is exactly what I chose to do.

Not long after this, an older man came to the door of the gym and asked if the owner was around. I told him that I had not seen him in months. He went on to say that there were three months owing on the rent, and they would have to close the gym down unless he paid the outstanding amount. My heart dropped. I had put everything I had into this gym, sacrificed so much, and now, out of the blue, it was over. I managed to contact the owner, and he assured me the rent would be paid, but after a month of postponing the inevitable, the landlords returned and said that he had not, in fact, paid anything.

During this process, I had built up some rapport with the landlords and was on quite good terms with them, so when I received a phone call from the owner asking if I would like to buy the gym, I thought to myself, why not? I knew God wanted me to be here, and I had an overwhelming confidence that defied logic about the place. At this point the owner owed me around 10,000 dollars in wages and roughly the same in back rent. I needed advice, so I contacted a mentor of mine, Mr Anton Bekker, who is a lawyer and a very smart businessman and explained the situation to him. To which he replied, "Maybe I should invest in a gym." I laughed, assuming he was joking. In fact, he assured me, he wasn't. Later, he told me that when he wrote and messaged me, he felt as if God's hand wrote that, not him, and he would normally not do such a thing without first consulting his wife.

First order of business was negotiations. I was thrust into the deep end between the landlords and the gym owner, both of whom had their own issues which I had to learn to navigate. The second course I had done during the lock down was business negotiation. I was able to put these newfound skills into practice in real time, with high stakes. The gym owner had verbally agreed over the phone to trade the equipment in the gym to recover my losses in wages, which was good, but I needed it in writing. One lesson I learned in that particular course was, "the faintest ink remembers better than the greatest minds", and I knew there was a chance he would back flip on this agreement.

So, after speaking with Anton, we had a release document made up that would outline the agreement, but no surprise, the owner became unreachable. Meanwhile, the landlords proposed other ideas to keep me in the premises, but that meant I would inherit the debt of the previous owner. I was not okay with this. So, I began to look at other spaces, one of which was across the car park for roughly the same price. After a lot of back and forth with the landlords, I involved Anton to aid in the negotiations which helped tremendously. We came to an agreement which ensured we all came out okay in this situation. As the negotiations were ending and a date was being proposed for the initial takeover of the premises, the gym owner popped back up and agreed to sign the document, giving me the gym equipment. On the 1st of October, Kingdom Martial Arts was born. I chose the name Kingdom Martial Arts because this was not my gym, rather a gym that belonged to God and His kingdom. I was merely a steward for His will to be done in the gym.

My hobby of Martial Arts, interest in business, my thirst for knowledge, and my loyalty to the gym, and God, all prepared me for this moment. As I sit here writing this chapter, it is three months in, and the number of clients has increased fourfold. The income sees the rent being paid every month, and I am doing less and less handyman jobs as the business is now becoming viable and I am nearly earning a wage. The journey does not end here, though. My goal is to bring services that bring value to the community and run classes that amaze people and leave them feeling as if they are getting more than their money's worth. I want this place to be a light for God, where we invest in people's character, lift each other up, and build our community. I am so glad I up skilled during lock down, trained harder than I thought possible in the gym, gave everything I had to see the gym I would one day own become a better place.

Life's training was there, and I thank God every time I come in through the doors of Kingdom Martial Arts. Sometimes we don't realise that what we are doing now, is just training for the future.

So, if you were offered the opportunity of a lifetime, would you be ready to rumble?

CHAPTER 13

SHOOT YOUR SHOT

"You miss 100% of the shots you don't take."
Wayne Gretzky

For close to five years, I found myself heavily involved in community work. I spent most of my evenings managing a creative space in the heart of my old neighbourhood. The space was a social enterprise that raised money to support mentoring programs for the more vulnerable youth in the area. Through working with this amazing organisation, I was exposed to many great opportunities that built me up and gifted me tools that later shaped my future.

I was delighted to be working alongside the biggest media production companies in the world, but at the same time I was disheartened. As you can imagine, I was rubbing shoulders with the famous, the influential, and the people behind the scenes who make it all happen. The organisation where I worked had several philosophies that we aimed to adhere to, one in particular was "SERVE".

The remarkable thing about this philosophy that I loved, was that life isn't about you. When we aim to serve a greater cause than ourselves, amazing things can come from this.

With every encounter with the who's who in the industry, we quickly learnt that if we could not serve the larger mission of our organisation, we were to take a back seat. While maintaining this attitude and discipline, I quickly noticed the people in charge began offering me more responsibility and more opportunities. It didn't take long to understand why the path to fame is filled with empty promises and broken dreams. With all the opportunities and promises I was given, very few actually followed through. Now, I could have taken this personally and said, "Well, fuck them", but instead, I took their kindhearted gestures and words of favour as nothing more than a compliment for the work I had done. Not only did this preserve my heart, but it also opened some space in my mind to see things from their point of view. Maybe, with everything going on at such a fast pace, they forgot what they had said, or they merely got caught up in the emotions of the day and offered something without giving it enough thought. Then again, in most cases, I chose to sit and wait and not shoot my shot by approaching them.

Some time passed, and our team was at a team building retreat. The boss decided we needed to do some bonding and a bit of upskilling to help us in our jobs. This, in fact, was an amazing opportunity and would become a pivotal moment in the trajectory of my life. There were guest speakers running short workshops and a psychiatrist talking with us about tools we can use to help the youth we were working with. Next, a somewhat mystical guru of sorts, who made us express ourselves through primal movements and find ourselves through deep eye gazing. There were others as well, but the next workshop was with a self-made Entrepreneur - a Mr. David Balestri who I would encounter again later in my life, who I introduced you to in the previous chapter.

Mr. Balestri was a well-dressed and well-groomed man at first glance, but as his long sleeve button-up shirt rode up his arm, there seemed to be a number of tattoos. "A past?" I thought to myself. As Mr. Balestri shared his story with us, I could not help but notice an overwhelming similarity between the two of us. He had grown up in housing commission, had real world experience of what the world can be like, the good and the bad. At first glance, many people could relate to this, but as he went on, he mentioned that, as a child, he would door knock around the neighbourhood, asking if people would like their car washed for extra cash, which my friends and I had also done. The more he talked, the more I listened. It was at this point that I saw someone I truly admired and wanted to emulate.

One of the things Mr. Balestri said towards the end of the workshop was, "If there is someone you look up to, ask to buy them a cup of coffee. The worst thing they can do is say no." Then, what he said next stuck in my brain. He said not to go to the meeting without preparation; think about what you would like to ask, and write it down, then take that with you. He said to do this so you do not waste their time or your own.

Several months, or maybe even a year passed, and I, as apprehensive as I was about contacting him, noticed him in the cafe I was sitting at. I noticed he was working, so I didn't disturb him and waited for him finish. As he closed his laptop, I mustered all the courage I had and approached him – I was about to shoot my shot.

To my delight, he was very welcoming. I asked if he remembered me from the workshop, and he responded with a vague, but polite, "Ahh, yes" I asked if I could buy him a cup of coffee some time. He promptly said yes, and we exchanged numbers.

So, taking Mr. Balestri's advice, I went back and started to write out the questions I wanted to ask him. One of which had to do with being a young man from the wrong side of the tracks, feeling out of place with my new standing as I began rise up the social ladder. I had a million and one questions but managed to narrow them down to a succinct few, touching on mindset, finances, and my overwhelming schedule of working several jobs and trying to run multiple companies simultaneously. Once I had formulated a series of questions, I felt he could shine some light on, I sent him a message and arranged a meeting. On the day, I asked if it was okay to take notes, to which he agreed. As I sat listening intently to what he shared with me, I realised he had given me the blueprint for the next steps I had to take.

I discussed this meeting with my partner, and she was very happy for me and affirmed that someday I would be in Mr. Balestri's seat, giving advice to a young man who needs some help. She went on to ask, "Are you going to meet him again?" To which I replied, "Not straight away". I wanted to implement everything he had taught me before contacting him again. For one, I wanted to show him that his words hadn't fallen on deaf ears, and also, that I appreciated the time I had with him, and thirdly, all too often we get all this great advice and never follow it.

Several months later, I revisited the notes I had taken from that meeting and decided to send Mr. Balestri a follow up message. This message was a summary of how I had put his advice into action and a thank you for his time.

Later on, I had a conversation with a mutual friend about my meeting with Mr. Balestri, and the first thing he asked was, "How much did he charge you?" To which I replied, "a cup of coffee". Shocked, he told me that it was usually quite expensive to meet with him. Then and there, I began to realise how lucky I truly was to have had an audience with this man.

Now, whenever I am faced with an opportunity to meet someone I would like to work with or just pick their brain, I jump at the opportunity. But I come prepared, so I am not wasting their time or my own. I often wonder what would have happened if I had called those people who offered me all those opportunities in the music and film industry. Where would I be now? I still, to this day, wonder if it's not too late to reconnect with them, years after the fact.

I have found great self-fulfilment in my life through building the relationships I have, and a lot of them have become quite fruitful. It's been a pleasure working with people I consider my friends and people I admire. There is always something you can learn from someone, so never be too quick to dismiss anybody, just because on the surface they may seem bland and unexciting. You never know, they may be the key to your success or just the conversation you need to pick you up.

CHAPTER 14

CLOSING WORDS

My life is far from perfect and at times, quite stressful, but in saying that, the lessons I have acquired in my short time on this earth have and continue to help me survive and even to thrive. I would love to tell you I am the most successful, happy, and greatest man alive, but the truth is I am full of flaws, shortcomings, and have a lot more growing to do as man, as a husband and a father.

This book was originally created for the people in my life who are yet to move forward in their lives, who find themselves falling victim to their vices and continue to tell me how I had it easy compared to them, as an excuse for their failings.

I hope this book is used as a guide to help people grow mentally, physically, and spiritually. I don't have all the answers and what works for me may not work for you, but I feel the things we have talked about in this book are universal truths that if applied, can improve our lives.

www.ingramcontent.com/pod-product-compliance
Lightning Source LLC
Chambersburg PA
CBHW061211070526
44583CB00025B/3199